MW00967189

His Voice
I Ier Words

OMARR ROBINSON

Yoshima Books

DEDICATION

This book is a 'Thank You' to my grandfather. His punishments of reading Huck Finn and many other books gave me a strong devotion to reading. He is gone but his teachings will burn bright and never be forgotten.

NOTE FROM THE AUTHOR

This book is a piece of work developed from my life. Through the ups and downs I have experienced from relationships, friendships and being a single parent, I am truly hopeful that each of you that read this book take something from it and are able to see something in yourself. See something in your own friendships, relationships, work lives and in the end are able to see my heart. I pray that each poem you read you are able to open up the door to your own heart and gain a sense of pride, humility or love. This book itself was brought about by the tremendous amount of love I have received from friends and family who thought I could do this even when I never thought I could.

The majority of these works are of a loving and romantic nature because we (men) don't open up our hearts and souls enough to our women to let them know how we feel about them. These beautiful queens are tired of always having to subtly express their own feelings to us and these poems are insights into their hearts and how they see us through their own eyes. Ladies, understand that men are stubborn but we do feel just as much love for you. Some of these works express how much we love and appreciate who you are, what you do for us and how much you sacrifice for us. I pray you all see that kind of love through these readings.

His Voice
Her Words

I am my OWN

Bewildered by the forest fog, seeing into the lights of all

I tried to reach to you with freight upon my haste

Can't catch you! Couldn't reach you! Wanted to see you!

I needed you!

I lived in a shadow of fear and pain,

Of darkness flowing through my veins

I wondered whose life besieged my own with a word of

Distrust that whispered in the air

Words of torment, words of torture, words of loneliness

Those words without an image,

An image without a face,

A face without a voice

Who's there in the shadows whispering to me?

Who's there controlling me?

Why do you not just leave me?

Darkness masks the light of day,

Truth of what must be part

Of my soul that is unreachable, untouchable, unknowable

You make me unknown,

This darkness screams from the shadows,

But no longer controls.

Allow my light to shine so bright,

Magnify and enhance my fight.

No voice, no pain, no more gain,

Bonds of the past will hold

No ground

Will freedom last through what I have found?

Trust

I've been waiting in this chill of a night

You told me that you would be by my side

I looked out for you day and night, through and through,

You were my strength, my armor, my guard

I believed in you,

In me,

In us,

In we

Now, what are we, am I, are you?

Where do I turn to from here?

Who do I turn to from here?

You said we were one, together, FOREVER

I believed in you, trusted in you,

Wanted in you

I fell in… I have lost myself inside of you

I don't know anymore,

I don't believe anymore

I am not sure anymore.

Can you show me more?

Give me more?

Do I deserve more?

Through the light a shadow of darkness

Unveils true destiny beneath my feet

Whose truth am I seeking?

Whose strength do I want?

Let me believe in you once more,

Let me trust in us,

Trust in you,

Trust in me again.

Whispers of a Dream

I see shadows in the moonlight

Whispers of her voice

Scent of who she was

Thoughts that roam and plague my mind

To close my eyes and cry of once was

To open my mind and dream of what could be

To speak about words that meant so much

A heart so alone, a spirit less than brightened

A voice muffled

For what is a voice without the one to speak of?

The shadow hovers over me

The whisper echoes loudly

Her scent over powers my will

How do I free myself?

Do I need to relinquish these reigns or

Hold on for a dream?

A dream of passion

A dream of joy

You are my dream

Dreams don't fade, dreams are stolen and forgotten

You are neither, but I no longer want shadows

Or whispers or scents

I dream and desire Truth

Your truth, my truth, God's truth is YOU.

Life

When I first awoke, your smile glistened so bright,

My heart filled with warmth

I looked into your eyes and knew I was safe from

My pain,

Your pain,

The world's pain

You touched my hand and wept a tear, for a tear

Of joy or a tear of sorrow, dare you ever share?

Will I stay with you for the rest of my life

Or will I be alone with another?

I just arrived, I am just here, the smell of

Fruit, the taste of sweets, the shine of brightness,

The sounds of all.

Where do I look? What do I see? What do I touch?

All I know is you! Do I know? Do you know me?

Aren't I with you? Will you have me?

Take me!

Hold me!

Kiss me!

Love me!

Grow with me, grow with we, we can grow

We will grow,

Together.

This place, a place of wonder, place of newness,

Thoughts, feelings, concepts, evils, and blessings

Brought me here, you brought me here

I love you, you love me, thank you for my life Mom.

Guiding Light

You were always there, you were always true

Your sense of strength shined greatly through

No fear, nor hate, or pain ever stopped you from

Achieving from day to day

You taught, you walked, you ran, and bought

You turned, and looked, and worked without a thought

Through strife and torture and arrogance way, you never

Ever gave in to say…

Your morals stood strong, your belief held high,

Your heart enlarged, your soul is on High

You were honest, you were true, no one ever knew

Can such courage reign supreme or is this all a fantasy?

I dreamt of you,

Looked up to you,

You guided my future too.

You were the center, the holster, the brick and the wall;

You held solid through it all

Teach me to read,

Teach me to trust,

Teach me to love,

Teach me, you must

Sorrow no more, tears all dry,

The smiles have come…

And I don't know why.

You are forever the mold, eternal as gold

Guide my life and I will always welcome your might.

Moonlight Dance

Dancing in the presence of the moonlight,

The stars shine so bright

Wind glistening through the trees

As whistles stream on leaves

The sounds of the lost, the sounds have found,

Where do I, or will I, ever get down

Go straight, go back, forward and left, right, up, down

I am all out of breath

Where do I turn?

Where do I look?

I have no light, I think I hear a creaking brook

Follow this sound, follow the tears,

The droplets on the ground, is nothing but fear

Run around the dark, search for the sky,

Your heart pounds and beats, as such clouds rumbling by

I see the clearing, there is nothing to fear,

But will I be found

Or lost for another year

Freedom rings, the bells atoll,

The joyous laughter of tippy toe

Come here, come to me, I want to see, and

Hear you all singing of glee

The loneliness, the quiet, the wind all around,

Am I truly back or lying in the ground

I thought I was loved, I thought I would be saved,

But all was lost for me, as soon as I heard *slave*

No more freedom, no more dance,

The howling of the night will forever be romanced

I pray for safety, I pray to be saved,

But it seems my prayers have died today

I will wait, I will strive, as the moonlight lives on

I know I shall not die.

Never Die

Love is strong, for your love is true, it shall never let me

Fall all the way through

I know who you are, you hide as if you're a ghost,

The mist you give is greater than most

Talk, walk, battle, strive, as anyone will,

We, with God can never die

We fear, we scream, we throw, and cry, but I promise

Heaven and I will forever thrive

We are partners, we are friends,

We are lovers to the bitter end.

Do we know, do we care, do we talk, or even share, do we

Wrestle, do we play, do we fight, at least one day

I tried to save, I tried to make it last, for our love I guess is

Just the past

I won't quit, I will strive,

For love and heaven will never die

To empower, too embroiled,

The love of you is supremely golden

Kids with laughter, the dog will play, the house is a wreck,

But I love you all day

God is my witness on that special day

He graced me with your presence, and I promised I'd stay

Never give up, never quit, that was our motto,

Now you say it!

For eternity I prayed, for life I begged, for days I wept,

For hours stayed

To love is great, to worry is pain,

I don't care anymore about holding myself sane

Give me peace, save my soul,

For life with you is breaking me whole

For I said as God as my witness, I say unto you forever

And ever… I LOVE YOU!

The Way Home

White as crystals, soft as sand, cold as the mountain tops,

The sounds of my hands

Peering through the trees it is so hard for me to see,

Where is my shelter?

Where are we?

Living in normality does not seem the same,

I thought I was home, I thought I knew this plane

Lost in the wilderness it seems as if,

The animals can't even sniff

I want my warmth, I want my family,

I thought I was home, but it seems I lost my sanity

The change in scenery, the brightness wares,

How do I find my way back to the land I once shared?

Do I ask for help, would I know where to go,

Who is even out in this blistering cold?

I listen for sounds of maybe a hound,

Or a whimper of a cat or something abound

I receive no relief or maybe a bite,

But I cannot be too far from my shelter of might

A place to rest, a place not so cold,

The chill in my spine and my toes seem made of stone

I am drowning every minute, with every passing mode,

I cannot help that I am now 60 years old

It seems I am no more, no longer bold,

My endo has given to this blistering cold

One foot, two feet, three feet, four,

No matter how much I push, I seem to get no more

Fight, push,

I say out loud, to the roof tops or

Maybe the sky is teasing me now.

A light of truth, or a light of safety,

I don't care except for saying HELP ME!

I am saved, I am not lost,

For this wind, this gust,

This everything mush,

It is not me.

It is not fun.

Why must every year, I work and deal with all this fuss?

New Days Beginning

The light of the sky,

The sun gleaming through a bushel of clouds,

A glint of shine that begins my day

A new of new, a new to start, a start of renewal

How do I renew? How do I begin? How do I refresh?

I begin with a blink, a flicker, a shuffle of my eyes

I look over and a sight of beauty besieged me,

A sight so bright, a sight of blistering light

Heavens hands, a graceful soul,

I can't imagine a sense that has overwhelmed me so

The softest touch, smoothest stride,

Oh, how my heart abides

A shape or figure, a foggy stare,

How I need to shake this blurry flare.

This day has given a new opportunity,

A new juncture in time

I beg and plead that all of this is not just in my mind

A face so smooth, a smile so angelic,

Eyes glistening with charm

The embodiment of a dream that has become a reality

Let my day, let me start, let me be joyous day after day

With this dream of dreams,

Bliss of bliss

Continue to grace my mind,

Blessing heart touch my soul with your daily presence.

A Blessing Sent from Above

Outstanding beauty, amazing grace, bewilders my heart

Without reluctant haste

Sky so bright, her heart so warm, I believe the sun is born

Her eyes gleam through the whispers of the night

Her hair so exuberant like a lake fire burning with rage

Her touch so soft, her lips so gentle,

To touch such lips again is all mental

I dream of such a touch, I dream of such a love,

To hear her, see her, touch her, and meet her

Is she a dream? Was she my imagination?

No, she cannot be

Because such a beauty is instrumental

Guide me through the graces of life,

Help see the wonders of joy,

Show me the beauty of the night

Awaken my heart, awaken my spirit, and

Awaken the laughter that has been subsided by demons

She is real, she is here…she is *you*

And you are forever near

Together with you, love doth not die

Friend in me, friend in you, lovers never wither

Our hearts are always true

Show me your smile to glisten away the sadness

Because all you are is an angel of happiness

Thank you, Dreams.

Thank you, Imagination.

You blessed me with an angel with such wonderful

Compassion.

Breathe

The air above, the air below

The breath I take keeps me whole.

The light of day, the black of night

I look upon your face to dismiss my fright.

A smell so sweet,

A touch so soft

I tend to wonder why my dreams seem so tough.

I was at peace, I was so strong

You stole my heart and now I am lost.

I thought I knew what I wanted.

I thought I knew who I was.

Your smile and grace destroyed my pace

I look anew and I looked for greater

Because

God gave a blessing so much greater.

I am stronger, I am wiser

I can breathe in the air

The bliss you share makes all things clear.

OMARR ROBINSON

Genie in a Bottle

Gracious day, a birthday delight,

Oh, how I want to kiss you tonight!

A day of joy, a day of peace,

A celebration that is never forsaken

I see you, you see me,

Your day is at hand

Shall we begin?

Child-like imaginations, child-like dreams,

Will you forget everything?

A year has come, today is old, when I look back

Was I truly this bold?

What have I done? Where have I gone?

The life of God is already won

Uplift me, believe in me, save me, pray for me, bless me,

Thank me

xxx

Be grateful with me, a day of new, a day yet again,

Oh, how could I ever spend?

Morning is dawn, the night is dusk,

A day of dreams have bewildered my mind

How do I free myself from this despair?

How do I grant my every wish?

A wish of peace, a wish of salvation,

A wish of truth, a wish of freedom

A day of wishes, a day of honor,

A day of selfishness.

I know such a day.

I believe in this day, I knew this day,

A child's day, a dreaming day,

A blissful day

Where have I gone?

Where have I been?

Come to me.

Return to me,

Be with me.

Take my love,

Take my trust, hold my faith,

Raise my spirit, guide my faith.

Your day has come,

Your day has arrived.

Be loved and blessed,

For we all must live and survive.

Future is Today

The passion we seek

The love that has come to pass,

Our hopes and dreams in life are

Sometimes broken like shattered glass.

We are lost.

We wander through the trees, listen to the wet leaves.

The sounds are confusing, I don't know where to go.

Until I hear a whisper on the air of your soothing voice.

The sound is faint but I know it well,

Your voice is like the sound Beethoven's concerto

The tone is melodic, the beat is very stern,

Please don't stop.

I beg.

I plead.

I am ready for this time of my life to burn.

You took me from that chaos.

You saved me from my past.

Allow me to show you what our future is like at last.

I was blessed with you, you blessed with me,

We are more than lovers, just wait and see.

Give me your hand,

You are now my wife, for our family starts today

And today begins my life.

The Lights Shadow

The Sinicism I knew

The distrust I embraced

The Lord's love I've always desired to taste

I was lost in darkness, a shadowy place

A place of silence, dreary, damp and cold chills

My shivers, my fears, my thoughts of screams

The horrors, the nightmares haunt all that I see

The life I only knew, where I never dreamt I wanted to go

You lead me astray with pleasures and riches untold

No more shadows, no more tales,

The only hope, the only light is the one upstairs

His words speak, his voice echoes, the tone rumbles,

The ground grows

The earth shakes with powerful rush,

My stability falters with every push and thrust

I am no longer blinded by the falters of frivolous things

I understand and see the true treasure

That lies up the stream

The current rushes fast and steady

Fast and steady

I'm trying so hard to keep the pace,

So all I do is stop and pray

I'm free from these shackles of restraint

No more tears, no more blood,

No more cries in the night of deaf ear's grace

I've been heard.

I've been freed.

My future now belongs to me.

BELIEVE

Eyes of dark, skin of light,

Sound of your heart cannot be eclipsed by fright

Hope of joy, your wonders grace,

Oh, how I want to taste

To be glorious, to be safe,

Your love is all it takes

I see through you

I see into you,

The fear, the pain, the sorrow,

There is no shame.

Don't you fear, don't you worry,

Allow me to stand next to you and marry

Bride of new, brides of old,

Oh, how you look bright as gold!

Your passion is true,

Your heart so tender, I wish,

I pray to have a plethora

Give me, allow me, let me try,

I beg and plead, do not make me cry!

I will kneel, I will speak,

I will ask you on the highest peak.

It won't be long, it won't be short but

I will promise to come back and be yours

No time to waste, no time can pass,

Let us fall into the blades of grass

I will arrive.

I will show that no matter where I go,

I will be here, I will be true

Your love, my love, is and will forever be…New.

Matrimony

My dreams of what once was…is *vanishing*

My future I thought I knew is gone

The love I had held so true

Vanished like vapor in the wind

The person I see before me is a stranger.

I don't recognize the person I hear around me

I can't understand the motions from who you are

Where is the person I knew?

Who is this person before me?

Can I go back?

Can I change the past?

The past strips us.

The past guides us.

I don't want that past.

Where is the future I was promised?

Where is the future I dreamt of?

Where is the family I pursued so diligently?

Come find me.

Come guide me.

Come show me.

Give me back what I lost.

Give me back what I worked for.

Make whole what has been broken.

Make right what was wronged.

Throw back this darkness,

This shadow of what I never wanted.

The screams I hear echoing are of my certainty.

Screams for my sanity.

Screams for my future.

I beg for my freedom.

Unchain me from the Hell.

Truth

What is this sense of reality in which we seek?

What is this dream of truth in which we yearn?

Sense of pride

Sense of hope

Sense of truth

Who's the one to persuade us to or from

The constraints of this shattered world?

Can we be, shall we be, guided

Down the straight and narrow instead

Of this windy, oblivious, shadow of a mortal dream?

A world of confusion,

Fear and terror, besieges us all

Love, honor, and truth will free us from our constraints,

Restraints, pride's and prejudices.

To have a dream, to have hope, to have faith, belief,

Trust, honor, is to look into something that has not yet

Been spoken into words

To look into a light that has yet had a flicker of power,

The belief that no matter whose heart shall be

Touched by the truth

Who's truth?

What's the truth?

Where's this truth?

Truth of knowledge?

Faith?

Self?

A truth unknown, a word unspoken, a light unseen,

A glory untold

Who will share with me?

Who will share with we?

Who will be by my side?

I don't want to cry.

I shall not die.

Why Do We Do Anything

Why do we do anything in life?

We do it to show our love

We do it to show our trust

We do it because we need to

We do it because we must

Our lives are windy roads

Crackling down a barren highway,

No signs, no leads, no gates nor forks, but we live our lives

The morning dawns, sky is formed,

The darkness has passed and I can begin again

New beginnings, new truths, new wonders,

New youths, new hopes and dreams

I have always wondered what may besiege me

The light of day glares so bright,

A sun of passion destroyed the night

We fear what we do not know

We hate what we dare to fear but

What if we embrace what we dare to hate?

And fight what we dare to fear?

Strength of life

Strength in numbers

Strength in honor

Strength to ponder

Belief in the unknown, hold for life,

Time will come for our life's path.

Beauty of the Light

The dawn of day has given light to beauty

Darkened by night.

A new day has risen, a new star is created.

A sky of wonder, stars of brightness,

Life after life, eternity after eternity,

Doth a thought of hope,

A dream of compassion, an empowerment of purity,

A strength of encouragement

A day not like any other, a day none like before,

A day of wanders, a day of joyousness

Allow us to open our eyes, our minds and our hearts

To the possibilities of what may await us,

Of the life in which we can partake

And show us each life, one life, many lives,

Intersecting, crisscrossing,

Intertwined by coincidence or fate,

By love or destiny

Give this day, one day, new meaning,

A day of restoration, a day of undenounced,

Uncontrollable,

Un-recanting, blissful…passion.

Life of a star, life of a world, life of a day

Can overtake the darkness of the night sky

Allow us to see the brightness that was foreshadowed

Before us,

Allow us to see the future in front of us

Allow us to see the love you hold in us

Allow us to breathe the life you have in us.

Dream Upon a Dream

I've dreamt upon strolling on a stream

Just to feel a springtime breeze

I dream of flopping upon the sand

To touch the earth

As though it were the softness of feathers

I dream of looking to the sky

To gaze upon a sun that shines so bright,

The rays of light stream through the darkness of my fright

I dream to see the air dance through the blue clear air

As though playing to a tune of Melodic symphony

I dream of a scent that enriches my soul with its lavender,

Berry, sunflower stronghold

The scent overwhelms my mind and

Fades away to a world of such a dream

I pray I could stay

To believe in such a dream is to believe in eternity

To touch such a dream is to have love

Where time is lost with the dancing sky

To live in a dream is to find peace of mind.

Quit

Can you fight?

Can you win?

Will you be the greatest that has ever been?

Your eye is so of the tiger, so let me see you soar

Throw that punch to the left and right and

Hear the crowd roar

The screams are deafening

The louder they get with every blow from you,

Don't you dare drop and quit

I believe in your might,

I believe in your power

Take my strength now, so you can go shower

It is ended

It is over

The fight has deceased

Your enemy, your bully,

Your nemesis is no longer on his feet

I am proud, so I applaud

Take a bow and hear the cheer

For you just might have a future graduating college,

My dear

Show no mercy, show no fright,

The world we live in only knows how to bite

Give them that left, show them that right

For you will succeed

Because I will stand strong with you and scream

FIGHT, FIGHT, FIGHT!

Years Never Lie

The distance between

The line of division

The thoughts that separate us from being embroiled

I've dreamt of you before I knew you

I've spoken to you before I heard you

You aren't new to me but where are you?

We are strangers, aren't we?

Strangers in the night or long lost friends?

Ten years have passed and we are starting over again

I've seen your smile

I've lusted upon your face

A lover's look I once embraced

I've held your hand that faithful day

Ten years gone and I am ashamed

We were best friends, lovers, and mates

Why now?

When did this happen?

These are all questions I want to erase

Come back

Come anew

For that love I had is not just tabula rasa

Ten years passed and I love you more

Give me ten more and I will adore

My best friend, my lover, my wife

I looked at you and I knew what was meant for my life

Shall This Last Forever?

You said you wanted forever.

You said you desired not just *whatever*.

When I asked, you said, "Never."

What was I thinking?

What were your thoughts?

I thought I understood our place?

Did you read the look upon my face?

You saw the love I had to give you.

You saw my soul shine and desiring to share.

You saw how much you made me whole.

I saw your look that first night I touched your lips.

I saw your expression the next night in wedded bliss.

I never thought me asking would bring regression.

Our lives were to be one, or I thought it so

Our lives were to be solid.

It seems we are to be departed.

You said you loved me, but I guess it wasn't enough

For I thought love was sacred for both of us.

I was in love with your soul, not just your body and mind.

For everything that was within in me,

I wanted to give to you in time.

I wanted a chance, I wanted a moment

Thought we had a shot until it was broken.

March 7th, 2:13pm, is a time that will never be stolen

You will always be there, you can never dissipate

For a love so true, it could only belong to you.

The Question

The breeze of the brush

The swish and the howl

So many parades of sounds

We walk and feel the sand between our toes with a cool

Push of water bathing beneath our soles

The sky so clear, a light so blue,

I frame this picture of me and you

This moment is frozen, this day set still

I can never forget the second you made me *feel*

You smile look so amazed I had no choice,

But to stop and gaze,

My question quickly asked with hopes and

Dreams set ablaze

Our future sealed, life has begun

For this day will always be the one

My life forever changed, yours will be too

For today is the day, I will marry you

I will make you my queen and I, your king,

For our lives can truly begin

Our prince and princess will know love like no other

For with you and your heart,

Only you can protect them like a mother

I shall fight and sweat and work needlessly for you my love

For today of all days, I feel I can fly above the clouds.

Young Man

Forgotten and lost

Darkness and out of sight

You pushed me down and tried

So hard to steal my might

You swung and cursed

Yelled and screamed

Took everything from me

I felt so little, beneath the dirt and sand

I had no life left, all I had was my son in hand

His life, his breath, the *beat beat beat* against his chest,

His strength, laid to waste this pitiful disgrace

I am a father, I am a man

I am standing tall and taking a stand

We will thrive, just he and I

For with him, I will always feel ALIVE.

My Nightmare

The screaming, the yelling

The beatings, oh my

The tears

Day to day

Never run dry

The running, the fears

There is no one to hear

The pleading, the begging, "Please stop, dear!"

I am sorry I upset you

I am sorry I am late

Here is your plate

Your bath is made

The kids are away

Go rest and I will be down and stay

Don't worry, you won't be disturbed for

I know the consequences from us being heard

I hope you are happy

Please sleep well for tomorrow

Begins a new day in hell.

Husband and Wife

The future is bright

I sense so many things

Such as a wife or husband for thee

The difference that makes a relationship true is the

Honesty

And lack of betrayal between me and you

I desire a wife

A wife who is honest and true

A wife who loves kids and playtime

Well, playtime at night just between us two

I desire a wife who loves my dorkiness

One who knows how to laugh and sometimes be serious

A wife who can cook and clean

Though, she must know how to jam to Billy Jean

She will love our kids and God in tow

HIS VOICE HER WORDS

For that passion of hers will spread from stern to bow

This is my desire, now let me tell you hers

For a husband she wants a real man she deserves

A husband with the arms and chest of a beast

With the heart of a lion and the touch of a sheep

Orotund and powerful, yet gentle and loving

He will know all her needs without someone telling

A husband who is honest and true

For his love of man can't be outdone for his love of God

A man so righteous and pure in spirit

He laughs and cries with her even though

He doesn't understand at all

His devotion to his family is never questioned

For this is her husband

Her man, her love,

Her very best friend.

The Time Has Come

A lifetime of dreams

A moment of thoughts

A second of pauses

A brief period of amazements

The ooh's and ahh's of life

The wow's and gasps of air

I knew you months before you were here

I saw you stir, felt you near

Loved you before I knew your name

I prepped, I cleaned, organized and steamed

I saved and moved and almost set the house ablaze

I wanted you for eternity

I asked for you in my prayers

My dreams of a future with you were oh so very near

The moment has come

The day has arisen

The hours tick down

Tick Tock Tick Tock

The moves, the curses, the tears and moans

The running, the screams, the drugs (oh my)

I am impatient, I know I must wait but this our first date

You are finally here

I see you covered in goo

I don't care you are my baby

WOO HOO!

My baby boy, my baby boy of joy

Bring on sleepless nights and screams of horror

Midnight feedings and hospital readings

The traps and the breaks, the ouches and scrapes

My son is here and I say every day…Thanks!

Passing the Time

Oceans of blue

Wells of black

Lakes of red

Streams of green

Winds that gust

Tears that gleam

Sun shines on two different fronts

Your smile seen in the moonlight sky

You are there, I am here but I feel as though we are near

No mountains covered in snow

Land blistered with sand

No rain nor wisps of air could keep my hand

From your grace

No more tears, no more gazes,

No more suns and moonlit phases

No more storms, no more dunes

No more waiting for Love's afternoon

No more terminals or planes to travel abroad

For the time is now

I am ready for peace

I am coming to you my *aking* queen

Yesterday was the past,

Today is the future

Be ready for our hearts to beat and never again fester

Memories

You knew me as a child

I knew you as a youth

You saw me grow up as a bumbling, stumbling oaf

I listened to you speak from a whisper

To a standing ovation

From a pimple to a zit, a bag to a purse

You laughed at my first flirt

I laughed at your skirts tear

For that dance will be part of our memories and

Your embarrassing fear

We laughed and cried about our parent's choices

And when we finally threw our hats,

The separation soon came and put an end to it all

The sun and moon came and gone

The laughter and memories faded with each one

The rain came more frequent,

The days seemed darker

For I missed my partner who always made me ponder

You surprised me with a smile I had forgotten

Life is brighter today and yesterday is no longer

Times will always be rough, life will always be hard

When I know I have you, we always get to deal the cards

Red, White and Blue

All this hatred

All this fear

All this screaming in my ear

All the stories of shots and kills

All the murders of innocence sends chills

From drive-bys to suicides

From church bells that made me cry

From school kids who are still growing from birth

To the grown who were to rule this earth

From the preacher, thank you for the food

To the children dreaming and

Playing outside as they should

Across the way on the TV we were shocked and stayed

Glued

We were the audience as two were betrayed

The crashes on the roads as people were sniped

By irrationality, it brings nothing more than fright

Our leaders weep with frustration

No rules, no laws, no thoughts of a solution

A country of freedom ruled by Law #2

We are trapped in limbo

I guess our freedom is only a concept and won't do

The cowards took the easy way to the left

Not to answer for the calamity we now live with

The hatred, the fear, the arguments run amuck

The lies, the cries, the bellowing of those on high

We no longer trust, we no longer know what we stand for

You all have failed this great land

We, the people, no longer mean a thing

For our pursuit of happiness…

Is no more than a distant memory.

Thoughts of You

Dawn of the day

Light of something new

I opened my eyes and my first thought was you

You awakened my spirit

You trained my heart

To believe in life and love again

And everything sets us apart

The smiles and jeers everywhere we go

The fireworks and magic as though we are

Children playing at the fair or in the snow

This feeling is refreshing

I feel so alive

Waking up thinking of you, I shall not tell a lie

All day long you race and tread through my mind

Trying to concentrate on work is not divine

I think about your touch or that giggle when you blush

Or that little wrinkle around your nose

When you laugh or fuss

That tone in your voice when you are annoyed

Or the soft sound of sweet tender snore

I love all the things that make you who you are

For they melt my heart and take away my frown

Your light is bright

Your heart so pure

Don't change who you are

For I know our relationship will endure.

Moments

At that moment I knew it was true

At that moment I heard from you

At that moment I could feel again

At that moment I was no longer last

A heart sunk

A spirit spoken

A body weak

An all but lost feeling of loneliness

To be thrown away as though not looked up at all

To be forgotten and left as if it meant nothing to you

We were to last

We were the future

At that moment you left

At that moment you walked away

At that moment I saw no future

At that moment he spoke to me

A moment of warmth

A moment of bliss

A moment of comfort

A whisper to a broken shell

All the pieces brought back from Hell

A life no longer torn

A future with new perspective

Hope of love now and forever more

FOREVER

Love is strong, for your love is true,

It shall never let me fall all the way through

I know who you are, you hide as if you're a ghost,

The mist you give is greater than most

Talk, walk, battle, strive, as anyone will,

We, with God, can never die

We fear, we scream, we throw and cry, but

I promise Heaven and I will forever thrive

We are partners, we are friends,

We are lovers to the bitter end

Do we know, do we care, do we talk, or even share,

Do we wrestle,

Do we play, do we fight, at least once day

I tried to save, I tried to make it last,

For our love I guess is just the past

HIS VOICE HER WORDS

I won't quit, I will strive, for love and heaven will never die

Too empowered, too embroiled,

The love of you is supremely golden

Kids with laughter, the dog will play,

The house is a wreck but I love you all day

God is my witness on that special day,

He graced me with your presence and I promised I'd stay

Never give up, never quit, that was our motto,

Now I want you to say it!!!

For eternity I prayed, for life I begged,

For days I wept, for hours, stayed

To love is great, to worry is pain,

I don't care anymore about holding myself sane

Give me peace, save my soul,

For life with you is breaking me whole

For I said as God as my witness,

I say unto you forever and ever I LOVE YOU!!!!

The Forgotten

Lost amongst the crowd

Voice shrouded with no sound

Face unrecognized by the people

Eyes looking bewildered

Blind to the fame

Deaf and cannot explain

Walk these halls with no view in sight

In this class and the future is not bright

To get in, to be in

To be seen as the king or queen

To be ousted or be spotted

To be known or just be shown

My name is…

I am here

I am not invisible

I am not forgotten

I am one of you

I am with you

Hear my voice, let me be heard

See my face, let me showcase

Look into my eyes, let me mesmerize

I am the future

I am part of the class of…

Pride

Sights and sounds

Manic all around

Running, crying screams make up everything around

Pushing, punching, breathing heavily,

I see so much depravity

They work feverishly and without praise

Many run in a blaze

They rush, they hurry

They prep and they shall not dare

Let not a single one disappear

They save, they risk,

They are always there

We look and stare and comment like we dare

We take for granted, when we should all care

They fight for us, take the chances,

They have families themselves

We all need to say thank you and

The city give them chances

Give them their worth, give them what they need

For without them my home, my life would not be

I will say Thank You,

I will give you praise,

For if I had more than that I would share today

They are the men and woman in uniform

They are all bold and stand true,

You deserve so much more but

All I can give you is a salute.

OMARR ROBINSON

Sound of Music

I heard a song so angelic

I thought it could not be true

The music, melody and sound

Warmed my heart through and through

The tone so graceful

The harmony so appeasing

I must find this person breathing

I hunt and search and dance through the streets

Searching and peering while people laugh at me

I pay them no mind for I must find this angel

I have never heard such a damsel

Her words with every passing note touches my soul

And gives me hope

I need to know who this is and speak to her

I am getting closer, the sound is encompassing

HIS VOICE HER WORDS

The sound echoes all around

I see her

I found her

There she goes

Sitting upstairs on a perch, I hope

"My lady," I yell,

"Please sing to me your music.

Your melody brings life to thee!"

She sings for me as I listen so deep

I fall in love with a stranger but this must be fate

My life is hers and we must not waste

Take my heart, take my soul into your music and

Never give it away.

Savagery & Grace

We fought

We cried

We bled for our pride

We picked and cleaned, bathed and steamed

Took the beatings and

Apologized for interrupting your dreams

Women raped, children taken

Men holding onto anger, such has been forsaken

Spirits held together with Psalms and hopes of freedom

People took us away on trackless roads

Dirt and filth, waterless ways

No one cared because we could not stay

Families broken yet they all prayed

Prayers of hope, prayers of freedom

Prayers so loud everyone could hear them

HIS VOICE HER WORDS

The road still so dark

Yet I see a light near the end and feel my heart

Breath of relief, sense of life

A new beginning without fright

No more pain, back-stabbing whippings

No more of that cotton picking collection

They make their new way, set up and free

This is how it was meant to be.

Underground to Freedom

Time has come

Time has passed

For the generations of beatings, cries and rapes are crass

The pickings, the shovels, the builds and the plows

The moving, the sweeps, the ma'am's and the howls

From shelters to cots, from the deepest chills and colds

No roofs, no clothes, not even one who is bold

Voices that yell, the blood that has stained

Your clothes have come from the pricks of the slain

The whistles of echoes

The sun's sweltering gaze

Our work never done til the day is a haze

Faith held us together

HIS VOICE HER WORDS

Hope shall set us free

For tomorrow or the next, this will no longer be

Wisp away in the day and trek through the night

Through water, forest, sand, mud and dirt

I will no longer be controlled by fright

I will be strong, I will have my will

My sons, daughters, friends and family

Will all know my thrill

The days of bombardments, the nights of restraints

I refuse to allow this to happen one more long day

I will have my freedom with tastes of tea

I am free by the sand or by the sea

I am done saying *Massa*, I am slave no more

I am a man now and all the further generations forward.

OMARR ROBINSON

Same but Never Equal

What makes us different?

What makes you better?

What makes you smarter, prettier, more deserving?

We came from the same streets

We came from the same hood

We came from the same beatings and

Run-ins where the Crips and Bloods stood

We were inspired by the same people

My friends were yours too

My family was yours

They laughed and cried right along with you

When you lost yours

When we barely knew

I fought for you

You fought for me

HIS VOICE HER WORDS

What makes us so different?

Nothing that I can see

I am darker than you

You are lighter than me

We are the exact same as we can possibly be

Why do I always get stopped, frisked and harassed?

Why must I feel like the child that no one ever asks?

Why do you get the pass and are looked at with such

Admiration?

You have the record and tattoos

This is me just dealing with contemplations

What do I need to change to be more like you?

Life is so hard in this world being darker than you

I am afraid of the street, I am afraid of the cops

For looking left or right, I may end up in a box

What must I do to get your kind of respect?

Never mind, all I can be is me!

Message from *Omarr Robinson*

I am a 33 year old single father from Hollywood, California. I currently reside in Atlanta, GA, working as a paralegal. I have lived in Atlanta since 1995 and have migrated between both Atlanta and California ever since. I have been writing poetry and other works since I was around six years old and have had an affinity for writing, thanks to my grandfather. Poetry came so easy for me to understand and is now a great expression of my life into words. My favorite pastimes are sports, movies (all genres), spending time with my children, and watching anime. I look forward to the next year ahead where I have so much moving forward.

This book is a huge stepping stone for all that is to come. My main inspiration to continue to do anything is God, daughters and my son. Their light, their passion, their love of life is contagious and mesmerizing. My family, first and foremost, means everything to me and I will sacrifice anything for them. To the man in my life who decided to take in someone else's kid and raise him as his own, I say unto you, *Thank you*. Thank you for loving me. Thank you for teaching me what it means to be a man, what it means to be strong, respectable and how to fight for what you need to get. Thank you for being the man I can and will always look up to. Thank you for being my DAD!

My mother's will and her strength as a single mother raising two boys is my other inspiration. It inspires my life on how to be a parent and how to raise my kids. Watching her sacrifice, her determination and seeing that no matter how much she got beat up, she never quit. She is my will of fire. If anyone would like to leave any comments or ask any questions, you can find me on Facebook under Omarr Robinson.

Made in the USA
Charleston, SC
21 March 2016